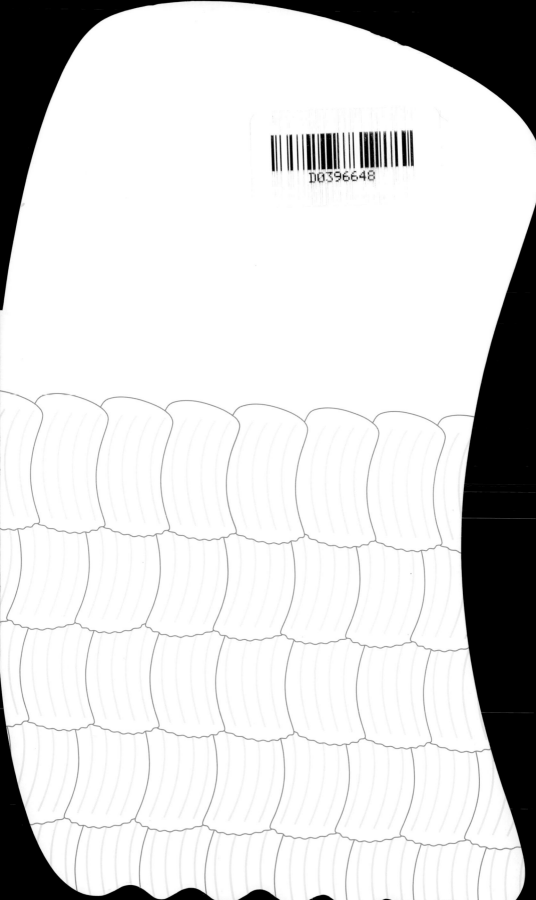

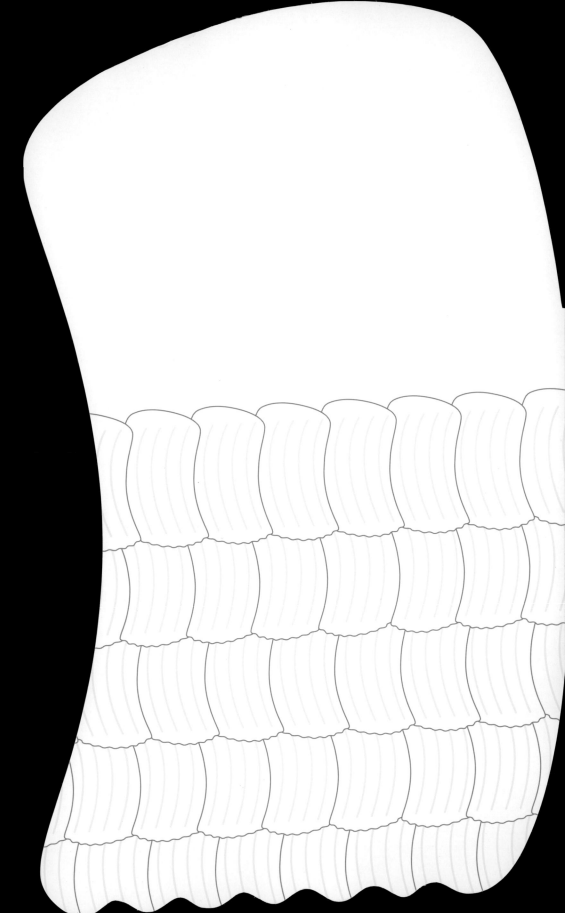

PASTA

50 Easy Recipes

ACADEMIA
BARILLA

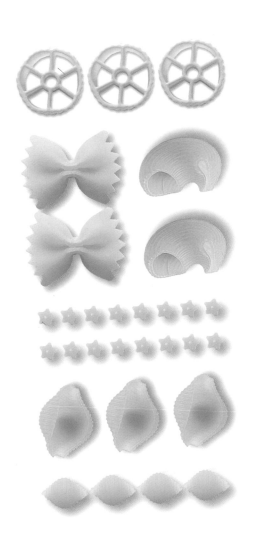

CREATED BY
ACADEMIA BARILLA

PHOTOGRAPHY BY
ALBERTO ROSSI
CHEF LUCA ZANGA

RECIPES BY
CHEF MARIO GRAZIA

TEXT BY
MARIAGRAZIA VILLA

GRAPHIC DESIGN
MARINELLA DEBERNARDI

EDITORIAL COORDINATION ACADEMIA BARILLA
CHATO MORANDI
ILARIA ROSSI
REBECCA PICKRELL

CONTENTS

4

5

PASTA
IS BARILLA

The fascinating and ancient history of pasta spans the length and width of Italy. From the first notes about fresh pasta dating from Etruscan and Roman times, to the medieval mentioning of dried pasta in Sicily, to Renaissance documents, and to the birth of pasta making corporations in Liguria and Naples, Italy is inextricably linked to pasta, progressively experiencing its transformations in which tastes and production technologies continually and reciprocally influence one another.

The history of pasta in Italy is closely linked with the history of the Barilla Company and with the family who gave its name to the company. In 1553 there is documentation regarding Ovidius Barilla as "Master of the White Art" in the city of Parma. His experience and skills were passed down from generation to generation, on to Pietro Barilla Sr., who set up shop selling bread and pasta in 1877 along the Strada Maestra di San Michele, making this the first nucleus of the enterprise of Barilla, today the world's leader of Italian pasta and ambassador of Italian gastronomy in over 100 countries.

This volume offers a collection of the main traditional recipes as presented by the company representing this product throughout the world.

PASTA: THE PRIDE AND JOY OF ITALY

... there was a whole mountain of grated Parmesan cheese, and on top of that were people doing nothing else besides making macaroni and ravioli and cooking them in capon broth, and then they threw them down to be scrambled for...

Giovanni Boccaccio, *Decameron*, day VIII, novella 3, 1349

Is there anything more inviting than a nice steaming hot plate of spaghetti? Is there anything more delicious than tortelli with its soft stuffing? Or more gentle and comforting than a broth filled with little pasta stars? Pasta is truly a it's own gastronomic world.

Who Invented Pasta?

As for all of the most successful inventions in the history of mankind, no one really knows who to thank for the invention of Pasta. However, one thing for certain is that it was not Marco Polo who brought pasta to the West on his return from China in 1295. It was already known and had been for quite some time. We have evidence, in fact, of a distant predecessor of pasta, called throughout the Eurasian continent, as far back as 10,000 years ago. Ever since man has been cultivating grains, he has been grinding, mixing with water kneading them and then baking or drying in the sun to preserve his concoctions.

It would appear that the Etruscans already had their hands in pasta dough, evidenced by some of the utensils found in their tombs, which are the very same utensils used today for homemade pasta production: the pastry board, rolling pin and wheel. The Romans knew about it too: from Varro who, in the first century BC, spoke of *lixulae*, an ancestor of our gnocchi, to the chef Apicius who, shortly after the time of Christ described the

lagane obtained from a water and flour dough then drawn and cut into strips, similar to our lasagne.

The First Historical Evidence of Dry Pasta Production

It is in Sicily, during the high Middle Ages, that we find the first historical evidence of dry pasta production on an artisanal and industrial scale. In Trabia, near Palermo, where a pasta was produced in the form of threads, called *itrya* (from the Arabic *itryah*, meaning "focaccia cut into strips"): it is described by Al-Idrisi, geographer to Roger II of Sicily, in 1154.

In the 1300s—after the production of pasta had spread from Sicily to Liguria and Campania, notably to Genoa and Naples and, later, reaching Puglia and Tuscany—the first pasta-making corporations were created and the forerunner of today's fork made its first appearance: that "pointed wooden utensil" suggested for use in eating the slippery boiling-hot pasta.

While throughout the rest of Europe people were still eating with their hands up until 1700s, the use of a specific utensil was proposed quite early on in Italy, for use in savouring the widespread dish of pasta.

9

Until the 1600s recipe books called for serving pasta as an accompaniment to other foods, especially meats, with prevailing tastes preferring it a little overcooked. Later on pasta affirmed itself as a dish in its own right, evolving to the point where today it tends to be served as a main dish, capable of providing not only carbohydrates but also, proteins and lipids.

National Glory

It was in Italy that pasta production became a real art. And it was during the early 1700s, with the first pasta producing companies and their rudimentary equipment, that Macaroni & Company became candidates for the Italian dish par excellence. Pasta became synonymous with simplicity and goodness.

Not only food for the poor but a delight to every palate, even the most refined. Even writer Filippo Tommaso Marinetti—in 1930 he launched a crusade against pasta in his *Manifesto della cucina futurista*, for supposedly weakening the spirit of Italians—once got "caught" devouring a fine plate of spaghetti at Biffi's restaurant in Milan. Before him, it was poet Giacomo Leopardi who had attempted, in 1835, to denigrate pasta, poking fun at the Neapolitans, who, he said, "were greedy for it." And the latter wasted no time in retorting, in rhyming Italian, that if the poet had loved macaroni more than books during his life, he would not have had such frail health or such a black mood.

Today pasta is the most popular dish in Italy. From the Sunday pasta dishes, still made by hand in many regions, to the *tajarin* of Le Langhe in Piedmont and the *pappardelle* of Tuscany; from the *passatelli* of Romagna to the *maccarrones* of Sardinia; from the *strascinati* of Basilicata to the *cappellacci* of Ferrara, and on to the most familiar shapes of dry pasta, from farfalle to fusilli; there are so many types of pasta that over 100 types can be counted up and down the peninsula.

Two Forkfuls in the Art

How many times has a dish of pasta entered into literature or Italian film? How could we forget Bengodi, the Land of Plenty described by Giovanni Boccaccio in his *Decameron*, where macaroni and raviolis cooked in capon broth came rolling merrily down a mountain of Parmesan cheese? And who does not get excited thinking back on Eduardo Scarpetta's *Miseria e nobiltà*, brought to the cinema by the Neapolitan comic Totò, who plays a penniless man so hungry that he fills his pockets with spaghetti? Or Mario Monicelli's *I soliti ignoti*, where the gang stops, while just about to carry off the heist of the century, to enjoy a plate of pasta e fagioli? And *Un americano a Roma* with Alberto Sordi, where the protagonist is a young man in love with the stars-and-stripes culture but can't give up the all-Italian pleasure of mom's delicious macaroni?

Dried Pasta, Fresh Pasta, Speciality Pasta

Pasta can be made at home with just a few simple tools: a pastry board, a rolling pin, a spatula and a knife (or the dough can be rolled out into sheets and cut using a special machine). The industrial production of pasta, however, is divided into six main stages: the grinding of the wheat (or other grain), mixing and kneading, extrusion, rolling, drying and cooling, and packaging. The "dried" pasta produced in Italy is made exclusively from durum wheat semolina and water (one method for determining the quality of such is assessment of the degree of transparency of the cooking water). Fresh pasta can also be produced using common (or bread) wheat and the dough can be rolled into sheets rather than being extruded.

Among the "special" pastas containing particular ingredients, fresh egg pasta, rich in flavour and particularly consistent after cooking, is the most popular. Naturally the flavour, colour, and aroma of a pasta will vary on the basis of the grain used and what is added to the dough. For example, we can make a green pasta by adding spinach; a red pasta by adding tomato concentrate or beets; orange, with carrots or squash; yellow with saffron or curry; brown by adding a pinch of cacao; or black using squid ink. The varieties are seemingly endless.

1001 Formats

There are long pastas and while some are round in cross section, such as vermicelli, or have holes in them, like ziti, others have rectangular cross sections, like trenette, or are a broad in width, such as reginette. There are pastas that come in nests or coils, some that are broad in width, like pappardelle, or of a narrower width, such as fettuccine.

Then there are short pastas, which can, actually, be relatively long, such as rigatoni or sedani, or of medium length, such as shells and ruote. There are the small pastas, such as anellini or tempestine, and filled pasta, like agnolotti and cappelletti, and other specially pastas, displaying the most bizarre of forms. Pastas can be smooth or ribbed: the former are appreciated for their lightness, the latter for their capacity to hold the sauce. Roughness and porosity, which depend on the means of production, are also factors to be considered when assessing the ability of a pasta to capture a sauce.

Cooking and Condiments

Pasta is generally cooked in boiling water. The golden rule is 1-10-100: 1 litre of water, salted with 10 g of salt, for 100 g of pasta. When the water comes to a boil, the pasta is immersed and cooked for the time indicated on the package, or no longer than required for an al dente texture. Cooking time, which can vary depending on format from a couple of minutes to nearly half an hour, is very important: it not only affects the digestibility of the pasta, but also its appeal. In order to keep the pasta from sticking together during cooking, it should be stirred from time to time. The heat should always be kept at a lively level and the pot, uncovered.

Once cooked, the pasta is mixed with the sauce. For recipes prepared with cold pasta, the pasta is cooked and drained while still quite al dente, then cooled by passing quickly under running cold water, drained again, then poured into a large bowl and dressed with a drizzle of olive oil to keep it from sticking while waiting for the dressing or sauce to be added.

For baked pastas such as timballi, the pasta is cooked to the halfway point by boiling, then drained, cooled, seasoned and baked to completion in the oven. As for the pasta frittata, typical of Neapolitan cuisine, the pasta is fried after boiling, then the egg and seasoning are added. In Puglia, there is the tradition of frying pasta in boiling oil, then adding it to the same type of pasta boiled in water.

The sauces that can be used for dressing the pasta are virtually unlimited. Ingredients, techniques and cooking times can all vary, from the classic Bolognese meat sauce to the timeless tomato sauce, from a creamy melted cheese sauce to a garden-fresh vegetable sauce.

Typical Dishes, and So Much More

Academia Barilla, an international centre dedicated to the diffusion of Italian gastronomy, has selected the 50 pasta-based recipes in this book. Some are typical of the Bel Paese cuisine and famous throughout the world, such as Penne alla Norma or Penne all'Arrabbiata, or the well-known Spaghetti alla Carbonara and Spaghetti alla Puttanesca, other first-course dishes were created by matching the pasta to ingredients from Italian gastronomic tradition: cheeses such as Gorgonzola or Pecorino Romano; or cured meats, such as speck or Parma ham; or the traditional balsamic vinegar from Modena; or mushrooms; or sun-dried tomatoes.

Sharing the desire to communicate, amid all the convivial spirit of pasta is what Italians are all about; in Italy—when you get to know someone and make friends—the question always comes down to: "How about we get together for some spaghetti?"

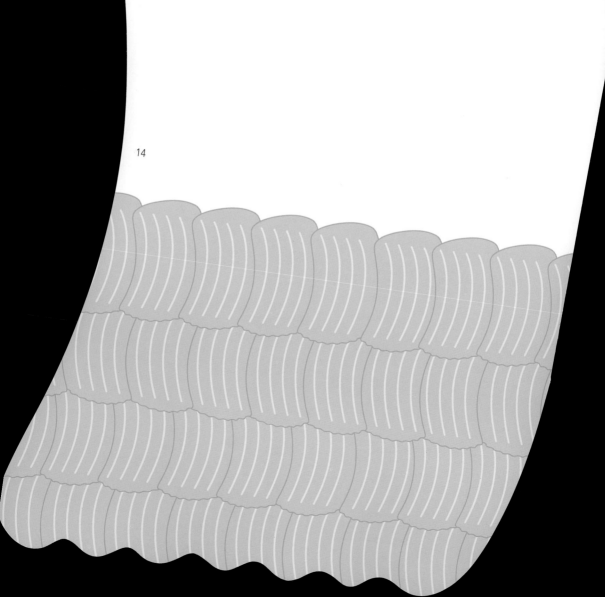

14

PASTA WITH VEGETABLES

BAVETTE
ALLA PUTTANESCA

INGREDIENTS FOR **4** PEOPLE

300 g (0.66 lb) bavette pasta
500 g (1.1 lb) peeled tomatoes, diced
50 g (1.76 oz) black olives, pitted
30 g (1 oz) salted capers
30 ml (2 tbsp) extra virgin olive oil
25 g (0.88 oz) anchovy fillets, in oil
1 or 2 garlic cloves to your taste
20 g (0.7 oz) parsley, chopped
1 red chilli, fresh or dried, to your taste
salt

METHOD

Brown the minced garlic in a pan with the oil, making sure it does not darken too much, then slice it. Add sliced fresh chilli or crumble in dried chilli wearing single-use gloves.
Rinse the capers under running water to remove the salt then chop coarsely with the anchovy.
Add the capers and anchovies to the garlic and continue cooking over a low heat for 2 minutes.
Increase the heat and add the tomatoes. Add salt to taste and continue cooking over a high heat for about 5 more minutes, stirring occasionally, and then add the halved olives (sliced if they are large ones).
Cook the pasta al dente in boiling salted water then drain and cover with the sauce and a sprinkling of parsley.
This recipe can also be used with spaghetti.

Preparation time: 30' + Cooking time: 6'
Difficulty: easy

CAVATELLI WITH FAVA BEAN CREAM AND CRISPY CRUMBS

INGREDIENTS FOR **4** PEOPLE

300 g (0.66 lb) cavatelli pasta
500 g (1.1 lb) fava beans (fresh or frozen)
100 g (3.5 oz) onion, chopped
100 g (3.5 oz) dry bread
50 ml (3 1/2 tbsp) extra virgin olive oil
1.5 l (6 1/3 cups) vegetable stock
salt

METHOD

Sauté the onion with one third of the oil. Add the blanched and peeled fava beans and gently sauté for a few minutes. Cover with the hot stock. Add salt to taste and let the fava beans cook for about half an hour. When cooked, blend to a thick cream. Crumble the dried bread in a pan and brown, with the remaining oil, until nice and crunchy.
Cook the pasta al dente in boiling salted water then drain and combine with the cream.
Sprinkle with the breadcrumbs and serve.
This recipe can also be used with orecchiette pasta.

18

Preparation time: 50' + Cooking time: 9'
Difficulty: easy

CELLENTANI
WITH TOMATO PESTO

INGREDIENTS FOR **4** PEOPLE

300 g (0.66 lb) cellentani pasta
800 g (1.76 lb) ripe tomatoes
60 g (2.1 oz) grated parmigiano-reggiano
30 g (1 oz) pine nuts
30 g (1 oz) peeled almonds
30 g (1 oz) walnuts
45 ml (3 1/4 tbsp) extra virgin olive oil
5 mint leaves
1 garlic clove, peeled and minced
salt and pepper

METHOD

Make an 'X' incision on the tomatoes and immerse them in boiling water for 30 or 40 seconds, then remove them with a slotted spoon and save the water for cooking the pasta. Allow the tomatoes to cool in cold water. When cool, peel and quarter them, remove the seeds and then cut them into cubes. Blend, to a smooth pesto mixture, the tomatoes, pine nuts, peeled almonds, walnuts, garlic, mint leaves, cheese and 2 tablespoons of oil then season to taste salt and freshly ground pepper. Bring the tomato water back to the boil, add a handful of coarse salt and cook the pasta al dente. Meanwhile, pour the pesto into a large bowl. Drain the pasta, add to the pesto, add a tablespoon of oil and mix thoroughly. Serve the pasta on individual plates. Add a drizzle of olive oil and, if desired, another sprinkling of freshly ground black pepper. This recipe can also be used with bavette pasta.

Preparation time: 5' + Cooking time: 10'
Difficulty: easy

FARFALLE WITH WHITE EGGPLANT SAUCE

INGREDIENTS FOR **4** PEOPLE

300 g (0.66 lb) farfalle (bowtie) pasta
700 g (1.54 lb) eggplant
30 ml (2 tbsp) extra virgin olive oil
oil for frying (optional)
1 bunch basil
salt and pepper

METHOD

Wash the eggplant then peel and cut into quite large pieces and boil in salted water for about 10 minutes or until softened.

Drain the eggplant and blend in a blender with the basil and a pinch of salt and pepper until it is a thick sauce.

Cook the pasta al dente in boiling salted water as per the packet instructions. While cooking the pasta warm the eggplant sauce over a medium heat, adding salt and pepper to taste.

Drain the pasta and add to the sauce. Add the extra virgin olive oil and sauté the pasta. Stir again and serve in pasta dishes. As a garnish try thinly sliced eggplant skin briefly fried in the sauté oil.

This recipe can also be used with fusilli pasta.

22

Preparation time: 15' + Cooking time: 12'
Difficulty: easy

FUSILLI WITH ARUGULA PESTO

INGREDIENTS FOR **4** PEOPLE

300 g (0.66 lb) fusilli bucati corti pasta
100 g (3.5 oz) arugula
20 g (0.7 oz) grated parmigiano-reggiano
10 g (0.3 oz) pine nuts
200 ml (3/4 cups + 1 1/2 tbsp) extra virgin olive oil
(preferably Ligurian)
1/4 garlic clove
salt

METHOD

Wash and dry the arugula then blend to a cream with 150 ml (2/3 cup) of oil, a pinch of salt, the garlic and the pine nuts. Add the grated cheese, to make a pesto. Cover with the remaining oil and set aside.
Cook the pasta al dente in boiling salted water then add to the pesto. Stir while diluting with a little cooking water and a drizzle of oil.
This recipe can also be used with farfalle (bowtie) pasta.

Preparation time: 15' + Cooking time: 10'
Difficulty: easy

WHOLE-GRAIN FUSILLI WITH PEAS

INGREDIENTS FOR 4 PEOPLE

300 g (0.66 lb) whole-grain fusilli pasta
500 g (1.1 lb) peas (fresh or frozen)
30 g (1 oz) onion
20 ml (1 tbsp + 1 tsp) extra virgin olive oil
salt

METHOD

Slice the onion and gently fry with the oil, until brown.
Add the peas and sauté together for 2 minutes.
Cover with 0.5 litres of water and allow to cook for
about 15 minutes. Salt lightly then set aside a ladleful of peas
and blend the rest until creamy and put back in the in the pan.
Cook the pasta al dente in boiling salted water, as per the
packet instructions, then drain and add to the pan with the
cream of peas and the whole peas previously set aside.
Mix all together over the heat for 1 minute and serve.
This recipe can also be used with farfalle (bowtie) pasta.

Preparation time: 15' + Cooking time: 11'
Difficulty: easy

MEDITERRANEAN-STYLE RUOTE SALAD

INGREDIENTS FOR 4 PEOPLE

300 g (0.66 lb) ruote pasta
200 g (0.44 lb) San Marzano tomatoes
80 g (2.8 oz) red bell pepper
80 g (2.8 oz) yellow bell pepper
80 g (2.8 oz) cucumber
50 g (1.76 oz) celery
50 g (1.76 oz) peas
100 g (3.5 oz) fava beans
40 g (1.41 oz) Tropea (red) onion
50 g (1.76 oz) black olives
20 g (0.7 oz) capers
80 ml (1/3 cup) extra virgin olive oil
oregano (optional)
salt

METHOD

Cook the pasta al dente in boiling salted water and stop the cooking by rinsing it quickly under cold running water then drain thoroughly. Put the pasta into a large bowl and drizzle with a little olive oil to prevent sticking. Blanch the peas in boiling salted water and cool immediately in iced water. Similarly, blanch and cool the fava beans then peel them. Rinse the capers and olives to remove their preserving liquids. Wash all the vegetables. Peel the onion and cucumber and remove the seeds from the cucumber. Cut all the vegetables into small cubes. Mix all the ingredients together with the pasta. Season with a pinch of salt and the extra virgin olive oil and then serve. Garnish with a sprinkling of oregano. This recipe can also be used with semolina gnocchi.

Preparation time: 15' + Cooking time: 8'
Difficulty: easy

ORECCHIETTE WITH TURNIP GREENS

INGREDIENTS FOR **4** PEOPLE
300 g (0.66 lb) orecchiette pasta
300 g (0.66 lb) turnip tops
60 ml (4 tbsp) extra virgin olive oil
2 anchovy fillets, in oil
1 red chilli
1 sliced garlic clove
salt and freshly ground pepper

METHOD

Wash the turnip tops, removing all the toughest parts of the stems. In a shallow frying pan, prepare a sauté with 3 tablespoons of the olive oil, the garlic, the whole chilli and the two anchovy fillets. Add 3 or 4 tablespoons of water. When the anchovies have dissolved, remove the pan from the heat.

Cook the pasta al dente in boiling salted water for about 7 or 8 minutes. Add the turnip tops and finish cooking together until the pasta is al dente. Reheat the sauté for 2 minutes before draining the pasta. Drain the pasta through a fine mesh strainer in order to retain the residue of the florets. Add the pasta to the anchovy sauce and mix thoroughly. Season with freshly ground black pepper and serve immediately.

This recipe can also be used with casarecce siciliane pasta.

Preparation time: 15' + Cooking time: 12'
Difficulty: easy

PENNE RIGATE ALL'ARRABBIATA

INGREDIENTS FOR **4** PEOPLE

300 g (0.66 lb) penne rigate pasta
600 g (1.3 lb) peeled and diced tomatoes
30 ml (2 tbsp) extra virgin olive oil
20 g (0.7 oz) parsley, chopped
2 sliced garlic cloves
1 red chilli, fresh or dried
salt

METHOD

Fry the garlic with the oil and chilli pepper (sliced if fresh or crumbled in if dried, using single-use gloves), taking care that they do not darken too much.
Once the garlic and chilli pepper have browned, add the tomatoes, season with salt and cook over a high heat for about 15 minutes, stirring occasionally.
Cook the pasta al dente in boiling salted water. Drain the pasta and cover with the prepared sauce, garnishing with a sprinkling of parsley.

This recipe can also be used with tortiglioni pasta.

Preparation time: 30' + Cooking time: 11'
Difficulty: easy

PIPE RIGATE WITH ARUGULA AND POTATOES

INGREDIENTS FOR **4** PEOPLE
300 g (0.66 lb) pipe rigate pasta
500 g (1.1 lb) potatoes
100 g (3.5 oz) diced tomatoes
80 g (2.8 oz) arugula
40 ml (3 tbsp) extra virgin olive oil
1 garlic clove, peeled and crushed
salt and pepper

METHOD
Wash the arugula. Peel and cut the potatoes in 1.5 cm (0.6 in) cubes. Cook the potatoes in boiling salted water. After about 4 or 5 minutes, add the pasta.
Meanwhile, briefly fry the garlic in 30 ml of olive oil. Add about 50 g (1.76 oz) of the arugula and sauté for 1 minute. Add the tomatoes, season with salt and pepper and lower the heat. When the pasta is cooked al dente, drain it and potatoes, then add them to the sauce. Mix well over heat for 2 minutes.
When serving, garnish with the remaining arugula and the remaining olive oil.
This recipe can also be used with medium shells pasta.

Preparation time: 20' + Cooking time: 12'
Difficulty: easy

REGINETTE
WITH MUSHROOMS

INGREDIENTS FOR 4 PEOPLE

300 g (0.66 lb) reginette pasta
400 g (0.88 lb) mixed wild mushrooms
30 ml (2 tbsp) extra virgin olive oil
20 g (0.7 oz) parsley, chopped
1 garlic clove, chopped
salt and pepper

METHOD

Wash and slice the mushrooms. Briefly sauté the garlic and parsley in the oil. Add the mushrooms and cook for about 5 minutes, making sure that the mushrooms remain firm. Season with salt and pepper. Cook the pasta al dente in boiling salted water. Drain and add to the mushrooms. Mix well over heat for a few minutes before serving. This recipe can also be used with mezze maniche rigate pasta.

Preparation time: 20' + Cooking time: 9'
Difficulty: easy

SPACCATELLE WITH VEGETABLE RAGOUT

INGREDIENTS FOR **4** PEOPLE

300 g (0.66 lb) spaccatelle pasta
200 g (0.44 lb) tomatoes
100 g (0.22 lb) eggplant
150 g (0.33 lb) zucchini
150 g (0.33 lb) red bell pepper
150 g (0.33 lb) yellow bell pepper
100 g (3.5 oz) carrots
50 g (1.76 oz) leeks
50 g (1.76 oz) celery
35 g (1.76 oz) shallots
50 ml (3 1/2 tbsp) extra virgin olive oil
4 or 5 basil leaves, coarsely chopped
salt

METHOD

38

Wash the vegetables. Cube the eggplant into cubes, set aside in a colander, add salt and allow to drain of its vegetable liquid. Cube the carrots, celery, bell peppers and zucchini. Slice the white part of the leek stalks and sauté in the oil with the celery and carrots. Add the rest of the vegetables (except the tomatoes) taking into account the different cooking times needed for each. Add salt to taste. Peel and cube the tomatoes, remove the seeds and add to the sauté mix. Continue cooking for a few more minutes. Add the basil. Cook the pasta al dente in boiling salted water then drain it. Pour the ragout over the pasta and serve.
This recipe can also be used with tortiglioni pasta.

Preparation time: 40' + Cooking time: 9'
Difficulty: medium

VERMICELLI WITH TOMATO SAUCE

INGREDIENTS FOR **4** PEOPLE

300 g (0.66 lb) vermicelli pasta
600 g (1.3 lb) tomatoes, peeled and diced
100 g (3.5 oz) onion, chopped
30 ml (2 tbsp) extra virgin olive oil
8 basil leaves, coarsely chopped
1 peeled garlic clove
salt, pepper

METHOD

Fry the onion and garlic with the oil until golden brown.
Add the tomatoes and season with salt and pepper. Cook
over a high heat for about 20 minutes, stirring occasionally.
Remove the garlic and add the basil.
Cook the pasta al dente in boiling salted water then drain.
Pour the sauce over the pasta and serve.
This recipe can also be used with spaghetti.

Preparation time: 30' + Cooking time: 13'
Difficulty: easy

VERMICELLINI WITH GARLIC, OLIVE OIL AND CHILLI

INGREDIENTS FOR **4** PEOPLE

300 g (0.66 lb) vermicellini pasta
70 ml (1/4 cup + 2 tsp) extra virgin olive oil
1 tsp parsley, chopped
1 garlic clove
1 red chilli
salt

METHOD

Cook the pasta al dente in boiling salted water. Meanwhile, peel and slice the garlic, slice the chilli and chop the parsley. Add the oil to shallow frying pan over a medium heat and allow to warm a little. After a few moments, add the garlic, parsley and chilli. Allow to brown slightly, then stop the cooking using a ladleful of water from the cooking pasta. Drain the pasta when cooked and sauté in the pan with the sauce. Serve immediately.
This recipe can also be used with spaghetti.

Preparation time: 10' + Cooking time: 11'
Difficulty: easy

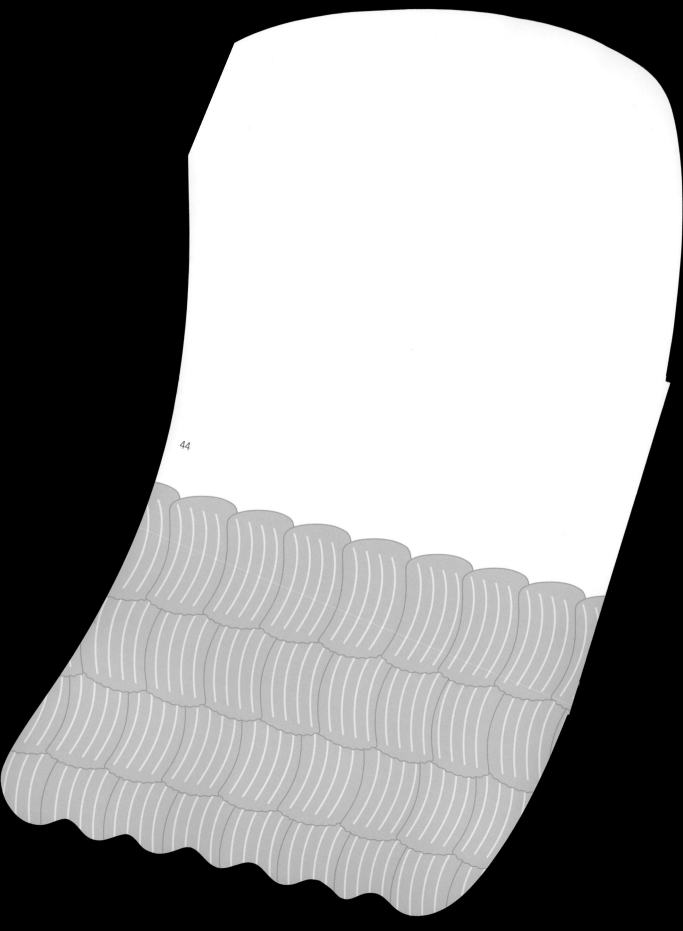

44

PASTA WITH FISH

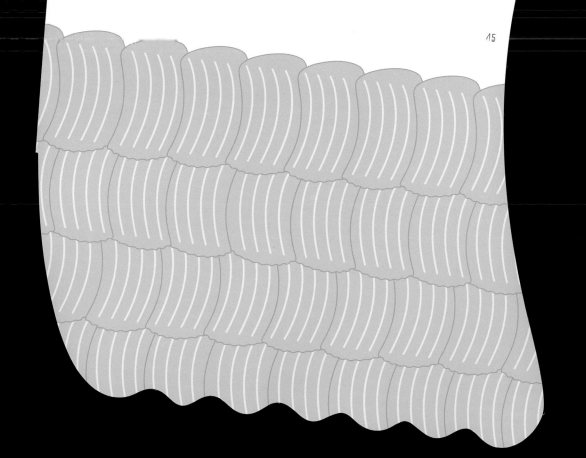

BAVETTINE
WITH CLAMS
IN WHITE SAUCE

INGREDIENTS FOR 4 PEOPLE

300 g (0.66 lb) bavettine pasta
1 kg (2.2 lb) clams
100 ml (1/3 cup + 1 1/2 tbsp) extra virgin olive oil
1 tbsp parsley, chopped
1 garlic clove, peeled and roughly chopped
salt and pepper

METHOD

Wash the clams thoroughly and place in a large frying pan
with a tablespoon of the oil.
Cover the pan with a lid and place on the heat. Sauté the
clams and when they have opened (after about 2 or 3
minutes), remove the pan from the heat and remove some of
the shells, leaving the clams and some of the shells
in the pan.
Filter the liquor, then pour this back into the pan with the
clams, and set the pan aside.
Gently fry the garlic in the remaining oil until lightly golden.
Add the clams and their liquor and heat until the liquid boils.
Season with salt and pepper to taste.
Meanwhile, cook the pasta al dente in boiling salted water
and drain but leave it a little watery.
Pour the clam sauce over the pasta and serve.
This recipe can also be used with spaghetti.

46

Preparation time: 20' + Cooking time: 6'
Difficulty: easy

CASARECCE SICILIANE WITH ANCHOVIES AND WILD FENNEL

INGREDIENTS FOR 4 PEOPLE

300 g (0.66 lb) casarecce siciliane pasta
200 g (0.44 lb) fresh anchovy fillets
30 ml (2 tbsp) extra virgin olive oil
2 sprigs of wild fennel, chopped
1 garlic clove
40 g (1.41 oz) apricots, dried
20 g (0.7 oz) pine nuts
20 g (0.7 oz) pistachios
30 g (1 oz) parsley, chopped
2 tbsp breadcrumbs
salt and pepper

METHOD

Toast the breadcrumbs in a tablespoon of the oil, using a non-stick pan. Gently sauté the anchovy fillets with the garlic in the remaining oil. Cook for 2 minutes then cut the apricots into strips and add to the anchovies. Cook for another minute then add the fennel, pine nuts, pistachios and parsley to the mix. After 30 seconds, remove from the heat, remove the garlic and set the sauce aside. Season with salt and pepper to taste.
Meanwhile, cook the pasta al dente in boiling salted water as per the packet instructions.
Drain and then sauté with the anchovy sauce.
Garnish with the toasted breadcrumbs and serve.
This recipe can also be used with sedanini rigati pasta.

48

Preparation time: 25' + Cooking time: 9'
Difficulty: medium

MEDIUM SHELLS WITH HAKE, FAVA BEANS AND OLIVES

INGREDIENTS FOR **4** PEOPLE

300 g (0.66 lb) medium shells pasta
250 g (0.55 lb) hake fillets, chopped
200 g (0.44 lb) fresh fava beans
200 g (0.44 lb) cherry tomatoes, quartered
50 g (1.76 oz) black olives, pitted and coarsely chopped
30 g (1 oz) onion, chopped
30 ml (2 tbsp) extra virgin olive oil
20 g (0.7 oz) parsley, chopped
4 basil leaves, roughly torn
1 garlic clove, peeled
salt and pepper

METHOD

Sauté the onion and garlic in the oil, until golden. Add the fish and sauté for 1 minute and then add the tomatoes. Season with salt and pepper. Blanch and peel the fava beans and add them to the sauce. Moisten with a ladleful of water and continue cooking for about 10 minutes and then add the olives.

Meanwhile, cook the pasta al dente in boiling salted water. Drain the pasta, add to the sauce and continue to sauté. Add the parsley and the basil. This recipe can also be used with tortiglioni pasta.

Preparation time: 50' + Cooking time: 12'
Difficulty: easy

FUSILLI WITH SALMON AND CHERRY TOMATOES

INGREDIENTS FOR **4 PEOPLE**

300 g (0.66 lb) fusilli pasta
450 g (1 lb) salmon fillets, skinned and cubed
300 g (0.66 lb) cherry tomatoes, halved
100 g (3.5 oz) onion, roughly chopped
30 ml (2 tbsp) extra virgin olive oil
salt and pepper

METHOD

Sauté the onion for 2 minutes over a low heat. Increase the heat and add the fish. Allow to brown for 2 minutes over a high heat. Season with salt and pepper.
Add the tomatoes. Cook for a further 5 minutes over a medium heat, moistening, if needed, with a ladleful of water. Season to taste with salt and pepper.
Meanwhile, cook the pasta al dente in boiling salted water as per the packet instructions.
Drain the pasta and add to the fish.
Sauté for 1 minute while mixing with the sauce.
This recipe can also be used with penne lisce pasta.

52

Preparation time: 20' + Cooking time: 11'
Difficulty: easy

GNOCCHETTI SARDI WITH GROUPER IN PIQUANT SAUCE

INGREDIENTS FOR **4** PEOPLE

300 g (0.66 lb) gnocchetti sardi pasta
250 g (0.55 lb) grouper fillets, skinned and cubed
450 g (1 lb) tomatoes, diced
30 ml (2 tbsp) extra virgin olive oil
1 garlic clove, chopped
1 red chilli, chopped
salt

METHOD

Sauté the garlic and chilli in the oil for about 30 seconds, taking care that the garlic does not become too dark, then add the fish. Stir and then season with a pinch of salt. As soon as the fish begins to brown, add the tomatoes. Mix and allow to cook for a few minutes. Season with salt. Meanwhile, cook the pasta al dente in boiling salted water as per the packet instructions.
Drain the pasta and add to the fish mixture.
Sauté for 1 minute while mixing with the sauce.
This recipe can also be used with penne rigate pasta.

54

Preparation time: 30' + Cooking time: 11'
Difficulty: easy

WHOLE-GRAIN PENNETTE SALAD WITH FRESH TUNA

INGREDIENTS FOR 4 PEOPLE

300 g (0.66 lb) whole-grain pennette pasta
300 g (066 lb) fresh tuna, cubed of side 2 cm (0.8 in)
200 g (0.44 lb) tomato, seeded and diced
150 g (0.33 lb) button mushrooms, sliced
100 g (3.5 oz) asparagus
60 ml (1/4 cup) extra virgin olive oil
1 garlic clove, peeled
oregano
salt and pepper

METHOD

Cook the pasta al dente in boiling salted water. Stop the cooking and cool by passing quickly under cold running water. Drain the pasta, pour into a large bowl and drizzle with oil to prevent sticking. Cut the asparagus to even lengths, peel the fibrous ends, tie into bunches and cook in boiling salted water, tips upward to prevent breaking, for 10 or 15 minutes. Stop the cooking while still firm. Drain and allow to cool then cut into halves, lengthwise, or into lozenges.
Sauté the tomatoes, mushrooms and garlic, in 1 tablespoon of oil, for 2 minutes. Season with salt and pepper.
Sauté the fish in 2 tablespoons of oil for 2 minutes, so that it remains pink.
Combine the fish with the pasta, asparagus, tomatoes and mushrooms.
Garnish with the remaining oil and a pinch of oregano then season with salt and pepper.
This recipe can also be used with mezze penne pasta.

Preparation time: 30' + Cooking time: 9'
Difficulty: medium

LINGUINE
WITH SEAFOOD

INGREDIENTS FOR 4 PEOPLE

300 g (0.66 lb) linguine pasta
400 g (0.88 lb) mussels
400 g (0.88 lb) clams
100 g (0.22 lb) calamari (squid), sliced into rings
4 shrimp tails (heads removed)
4 prawns
4 cuttlefish
150 g (0.33 lb) tomatoes, seeded and cut in strips
150 ml (2/3 cups) white wine
40 ml (3 tbsp) extra virgin olive oil
1 garlic clove
1 tbsp parsley, chopped
1 bunch basil, roughly torn
salt and pepper

METHOD

Wash the mussels and clams well and remove any sand.
Sauté the garlic, parsley and basil in the oil.
Add the mussels, clams and wine. Cover with a lid and allow
the heat to open the shells. As they open, remove them from
the pan. Remove about three-quarters of the shellfish from
their shells and set aside in a bowl. Add the calamari,
cuttlefish, prawns, shrimp tails and tomatoes. Sauté for
2 minutes, then add the previously set aside shellfish.
Season with salt and pepper. The sauce should retain
some of its liquidity.
Cook the pasta al dente in boiling salted water.
Drain the pasta, add to the sauce and sauté.
This recipe can also be used with bavette pasta.

MEZZE MANICHE RIGATE WITH CLAMS AND CHICKPEAS

INGREDIENTS FOR 4 PEOPLE

300 g (0.66 lb) mezze maniche rigate pasta
100 g (0.22 lb) dried chickpeas or 250 g (0.55 lb) pre-cooked chickpeas
800 g (1.76 lb) clams
20 g (0.7 oz) parsley, chopped
60 ml (1/4 cup) extra virgin olive oil
4 or 5 basil leaves, cut in thin strips
1 garlic clove, peeled
1 red chilli
salt and pepper

METHOD

Allow dried chickpeas, if used, to soak overnight (12 hours) but you can use canned, pre-cooked chickpeas instead.
Add the chickpeas to cold water and boil for about 1 hour, until soft. Meanwhile, sauté the garlic, chilli and parsley in half the oil until the garlic is light brown. Wash the clams well, add to the garlic and allow the heat to open them.
Once opened, filter the liquor and remove some of the shells.
When the chickpeas are cooked, drain and mash then moisten with a little of the clam liquor and the remaining olive oil. Season with a pinch of salt and freshly ground pepper.
Cook the pasta al dente in boiling salted water and drain.
Add the pasta and chickpeas to the clams and sauté with the clams. Add the basil and serve.
This recipe can also be used with rigatoni pasta.

Preparation time: 1 h + Cooking time: 12' + Soaking time: 12 h
Difficulty: medium

MEZZE MANICHE RIGATE WITH SEAFOOD AND MUSHROOMS

INGREDIENTS FOR 4 PEOPLE

300 g (0.66 lb) mezze maniche rigate pasta
20 shrimps
150 g (0.33 lb) fresh tuna or swordfish, cubed of side 1.5 cm (0.6 in)
200 g (0.44 lb) button mushrooms, sliced
100 g (3.5 oz) tomatoes, seeded and diced
60 ml (1/4 cup) extra virgin olive oil
20 g (0.7 oz) parsley, chopped
1 garlic clove, peeled and chopped
salt and pepper

METHOD

Clean and shell the shrimp (you can leave some of the shells on).
Cook the pasta al dente in boiling salted water.
Meanwhile, sear the tuna and shrimp for about 2 minutes in half the oil.
Season with salt and pepper and set aside. In the same pan, in the remaining oil, sauté the garlic and, before it starts turning golden brown, add the mushrooms. Sauté for 2 minutes then add the tomatoes. Continue cooking for another 2 minutes, adding, if necessary, a little of the pasta liquor. Add the shrimp and tuna.
Drain the pasta and add to the sauce.
Then add the parsley and sauté.
This recipe can also be used with penne rigate pasta.

Preparation time: 20' + Cooking time: 14'
Difficulty: easy

SEDANINI RIGATI WITH MUSSELS AND TOMATOES

INGREDIENTS FOR **4** PEOPLE

300 g (0.66 lb) sedanini rigati pasta
550 g (1.21 lb) tomatoes (on the vine)
800 g (1.76 lb) mussels
60 ml (1/4 cup) extra virgin olive oil
30 g (1 oz) onion, chopped
20 g (0.7 oz) parsley, chopped
4 or 5 basil leaves, chopped
1 garlic clove, peeled
1 red chilli
salt, pepper

METHOD

Lightly sauté the garlic, onion, chilli and parsley in the oil.
Wash the mussels and add to the garlic, allowing
them to open.
Once opened, filter the liquor and remove the shells. Blend
the tomatoes, seasoned with salt and pepper, and add this to
the mussel sauce. Cook the pasta al dente in boiling salted
water and drain.
Add the pasta and basil to the mussel sauce and sauté,
without cooking too much.
This recipe can also be used with mezze penne pasta.

Preparation time: 1 h + Cooking time: 12'
Difficulty: medium

SPAGHETTI WITH SQUID INK

INGREDIENTS FOR **4** PEOPLE

300 g (0.6 lb) spaghetti
400 g (0.88 lb) San Marzano tomatoes, seeded and diced
15 g (0.53 oz) squid ink
35 ml (2 1/2 tbsp) extra virgin olive oil
30 g (1 oz) parsley, chopped
1 garlic clove, peeled
1 red chilli, minced
salt

METHOD

Cook the pasta al dente in boiling salted water. Meanwhile, sauté the garlic, parsley (set aside a pinch as a garnish) and chilli for 1 minute, then add the tomatoes. Allow to cook for another minute, then add the squid ink and dilute with a ladleful of the pasta water. Allow to reduce slightly, over a low heat, for 2 or 3 minutes. Season with salt.
Drain the spaghetti and add to the garlic pan. Sauté, then garnish with the set aside parsley and serve.
This recipe can also be used with linguine pasta.

Preparation time: 5' + Cooking time: 8'
Difficulty: easy

WHOLE-GRAIN SPAGHETTI WITH PRAWNS

INGREDIENTS FOR 4 PEOPLE

300 g (0.66 lb) whole-grain spaghetti
12 prawns
200 g (0.44 lb) cherry tomatoes, cut in wedges
60 ml (1/4 cup) extra virgin olive oil
30 ml (2 tbsp) white wine
30 g (1 oz) parsley, chopped
1 garlic clove, peeled
1 red chilli
salt

METHOD

Sauté the garlic in half the oil. When it begins to turn golden brown, add the chilli and the prawns.
Sear quickly then add the wine. Once the wine has evaporated, add the tomatoes and cook for 5 minutes.
Season with salt and add the parsley.
Meanwhile, cook the pasta al dente in boiling salted water.
Drain, add to the prawns and sauté.
Add a little of the pasta liquor and the remaining oil.
This recipe can also be used with bavette pasta.

Preparation time: 20' + Cooking time: 8'
Difficulty: medium

SPAGHETTI WITH BOTTARGA

INGREDIENTS FOR **4** PEOPLE

300 g (0.66 lb) spaghetti
60 g (2.1 oz) bottarga, grated
100 ml (1/3 cup + 1 1/2 tbsp) extra virgin olive oil
1 garlic clove, peeled
salt and pepper

METHOD

Sauté the garlic in the oil over a medium heat, until oil takes on the flavour of the garlic.
Remove the pan from the heat before the garlic becomes toasted and remove the garlic. Season to taste with freshly ground pepper.
Add half the bottarga to the oil.
Cook the pasta al dente in boiling salted water. Drain the pasta, add the remaining oil and bottarga and mix thoroughly.
Serve the spaghetti in pasta dishes and sprinkle with the remaining bottarga.
This recipe can also be used with vermicellini pasta.
In case you do not find bottarga, blend 4 anchovy fillets with 4 tablespoons of olive oil, and 2 fistfuls of breadcrumbs.
Toast the mixture in a non-stick pan for 3-4 minutes, and proceed as previously described.

70

Preparation time: 5' + Cooking time: 11'
Difficulty: easy

TRENETTE WITH ZUCCHINI AND SMOKED SWORDFISH

INGREDIENTS FOR **4** PEOPLE

300 g (0.66 lb) trenette pasta
200 g (0.44 lb) zucchini, thinly sliced to 2 mm (0.08 in)
30 g (1 oz) shallots, chopped
160 g (0.35 lb) smoked swordfish
30 ml (2 tbsp) extra virgin olive oil
20 g (0.7 oz) parsley, chopped
zest of half a lemon
salt and pepper

METHOD

Cut the zucchini slices into small batons. Cut the fish into similar sized batons. Sauté the shallots in the oil, over a medium heat, until just brown. Increase the heat and add the zucchini. Sauté for 1 minute, then season with salt and pepper and remove from the heat. Add the fish. Add the lemon zest.
Cook the pasta al dente in boiling salted water as per the packet instructions.
Drain the pasta and add immediately to the sauce. Sauté, adding the parsley and, if necessary, a little of the pasta water.
This recipe can also be used with spaghettini pasta.

Preparation time: 15' + Cooking time: 8'
Difficulty: easy

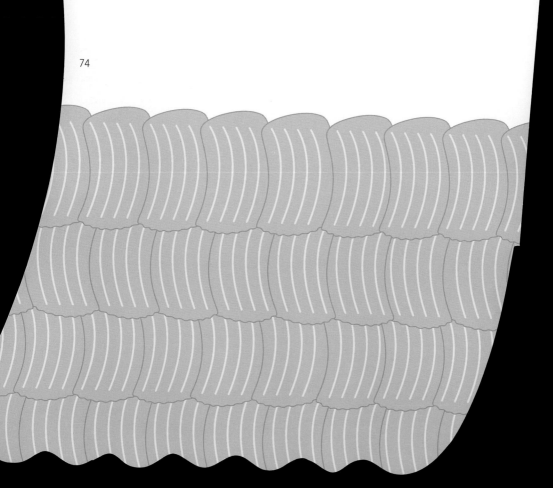

74

PASTA WITH MEAT

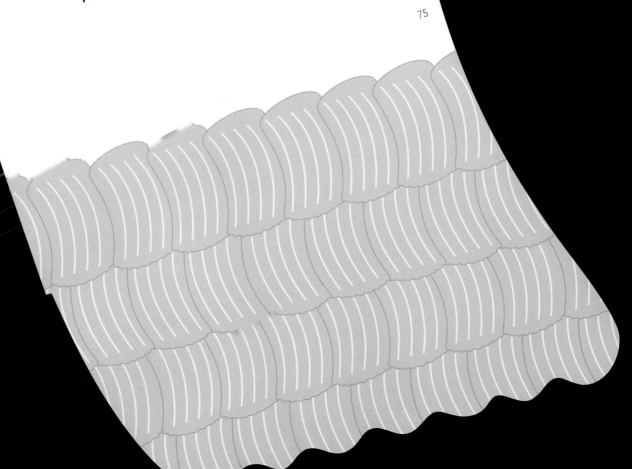

BUCATINI ALL'AMATRICIANA

INGREDIENTS FOR **4** PEOPLE

300 g (0.66 lb) bucatini pasta
400 g (0.88 lb) tomatoes, diced
150 g (0.33 lb) smoked pork jowl or bacon, sliced
40 g (1.41 oz) pecorino romano cheese, grated
1 red chilli, crumbled
salt and pepper

METHOD

Cut the meat into strips and fry over a high heat, with a little water, to allow the fat to melt.
Remove the meat from the pan and set aside. Add the tomatoes, chilli, a pinch of salt and some ground pepper to the pan and cook for about 10 minutes. Add the previously set aside meat to the sauce and reheat.
Meanwhile, cook the pasta al dente in boiling salted water. Drain the pasta and mix with the sauce and the grated cheese.
Mix well and serve hot.
This recipe can also be used with spaghetti.

Preparation time: 15' + Cooking time: 8'
Difficulty: easy

FUSILLI WITH SPECK AND RADICCHIO

INGREDIENTS FOR **4** PEOPLE

300 g (0.66 lb) fusilli pasta
30 ml (2 tbsp) extra virgin olive oil
250 g (0.55 lb) radicchio, cut in strips
120 g (0.26 lb) speck, cut in strips
150 ml (2/3 cup) full cream
40 g (1.41 oz) shallots, sliced
salt and pepper

METHOD

Sauté the shallots in the oil over a low heat and allow
to brown for 3 to 4 minutes.
Add the speck and sauté for another 2 to 3 minutes
over a medium heat.
Add the radicchio and cook for 5 minutes.
Add the cream and season with salt and pepper.
Reduce the sauce, if necessary, over a low heat.
Meanwhile, cook the pasta al dente in boiling salted water.
Drain the pasta and mix thoroughly with the sauce.
This recipe can also be used with sedani rigati pasta.

Preparation time: 20' + Cooking time: 12'
Difficulty: medium

GRAMIGNA
WITH SAUSAGE
AND BELL PEPPER SAUCE

INGREDIENTS FOR **4** PEOPLE

300 g (0.66 lb) gramigna pasta
300 g (0.66 lb) sausage
180 g (0.4 lb) onion, thinly sliced
300 g (0.66 lb) tomatoes, diced
100 g (3.5 oz) red bell pepper, seeded
100 g (3.5 oz) yellow bell pepper, seeded
100 g (3.5 oz) black olives
60 ml (1/4 cup) extra virgin olive oil
salt and pepper

METHOD

Sauté the onion in half the oil until brown. Cut the peppers
into lozenge shapes and add to the onion.
Remove the sausage skin and crumble the sausage into
another pan and sauté with the remaining oil.
When nicely browned, pour off the melted fat and
add the sausage to the pepper mix.
Add the tomatoes and season with salt and pepper.
Continue cooking for another 15 minutes
and then add the olives.
Cook the pasta al dente in boiling salted water.
Drain the pasta and mix with the sauce.
This recipe can also be used with tortiglioni pasta.

Preparation time: 30' + Cooking time: 5'
Difficulty: medium

PENNE LISCE WITH SQUASH AND PANCETTA

INGREDIENTS FOR 4 PEOPLE

300 g (0.66 lb) penne lisce pasta
650 g (1.43 lb) squash, peeled and cubed of side 1 cm (0.4 in)
200 g (0.44 lb) pancetta (cured pork), thinly sliced
50 g (1.76 oz) onion, chopped
25 g (1 3/4 tbsp) butter
thyme
salt and pepper

METHOD

From cold, boil half the squash cubes, the onion and a pinch of salt. When cooked, blend to a cream.
Allow the meat to dry in an oven at 150°C (300°F) for about 15 minutes, until crunchy.
Sauté the thyme in the butter over a medium heat.
Add the remaining squash cubes and sauté.
Season to taste with salt and pepper.
Add the previously prepared squash cream.
Cook the pasta al dente in boiling salted water.
Drain the pasta, add to the sauce and sauté together.
Serve in pasta dishes and garnish with the crunchy pancetta.
This recipe can also be used with farfalle (bowtie) pasta.

Preparation time: 30' + Cooking time: 8'
Difficulty: easy

RIGATONI WITH SAUSAGE AND SAFFRON

INGREDIENTS FOR **4** PEOPLE

300 g (0.66 lb) rigatoni pasta
300 g (0.66 lb) sausage
150 g (0.33 lb) leeks, white part only, thinly sliced
150 ml (2/3 cup) full cream
60 ml (1/4 cup) extra virgin olive oil
0.5 g saffron
salt and pepper

METHOD

Gently sauté the leeks over a low heat with half the oil.
Meanwhile, remove the sausage skin and crumble the meat into a pan.
Sauté the meat with the remaining olive oil.
When nicely brown, pour off the melted fat and add the meat to the leeks.
Continue cooking for 5 minutes.
If the mixture becomes too dry add a few tablespoons of water.
Add the cream and saffron and season with salt and pepper. Keep warm.
Meanwhile, cook the pasta al dente in boiling salted water.
Drain the pasta and add to the sauce.
Mix well over a medium heat for 2 minutes before serving.
This recipe can also be used with orecchiette pasta.

Preparation time: 30' + Cooking time: 11'
Difficulty: medium

SEDANI RIGATI WITH PARMA HAM AND TRADITIONAL BALSAMIC VINEGAR

INGREDIENTS FOR **4 PEOPLE**

300 g (0.66 lb) sedani rigati pasta
120 g (0.26 lb) Parma ham, cut in strips of thickness 2-3 mm (0.08-0.11 in)
50 g (3 1/2 tbsp) butter
40 g (1.41 oz) parmigiano-reggiano cheese, flaked
40 ml (3 tbsp) Balsamic Vinegar Modena DOP
4 sprigs of thyme
salt

METHOD

Cook the pasta al dente in boiling salted water.
Meanwhile, melt the butter in a non-stick frying pan.
Add the ham and allow to brown for 2 minutes, then sprinkle
with the balsamic vinegar and continue cooking
for another 3 to 4 minutes, so that the sauce becomes
a little syrupy. Drain the pasta, add it to the sauce
with the leaves from the sprigs of thyme.
Serve in pasta dishes and garnish with cheese.
This recipe can also be used with penne rigate pasta.

Preparation time: 15' + Cooking time: 12'
Difficulty: easy

SPACCATELLE WITH MUSHROOMS, BRESAOLA AND ARUGULA

INGREDIENTS FOR 4 PEOPLE

300 g (0.66 lb) spaccatelle pasta
200 g (0.44 lb) button mushrooms, trimmed and sliced
200 ml (3/4 cup + 1 1/2 tbsp) full cream
100 g (3.5 oz) bresaola, cut in thin strips
100 g (3.5 oz) tomatoes, diced
50 g (1.76 oz) arugula, coarsely chopped
40 g (1.41 oz) parmigiano-reggiano cheese, grated
30 ml (2 tbsp) extra virgin olive oil
20 g (0.7 oz) parsley, chopped
1 garlic clove, peeled
salt and pepper

METHOD

Gently sauté the garlic, mushrooms and parsley in the oil
over a medium heat for 2 minutes.
Season with salt and pepper.
Add the bresaola, allow the flavours to mix for 2 seconds
and add the tomatoes.
Cook for 5 minutes over a high heat.
Add the cream then lower the heat and allow the sauce
to reduce for 2 to 3 minutes.
Season with salt and pepper.
Meanwhile, cook the pasta al dente in boiling salted water.
Drain the pasta, add to the sauce with the arugula and sauté.
Garnish with cheese and a few leaves of uncooked arugula
or a few slices of mushroom.
This recipe can also be used with casarecce pasta.

88

Preparation time: 50' + Cooking time: 9'
Difficulty: easy

SPAGHETTI ALLA CARBONARA

INGREDIENTS FOR **4** PEOPLE

300 g (0.66 lb) spaghetti
150 g (0.33 lb) cured pork jowl or cured pork (bacon), sliced
4 egg yolks
100 g (3.5 oz) pecorino romano cheese
salt and pepper

METHOD

Beat the egg yolks with a pinch of salt, black pepper
and a tablespoon of cheese.
Cut the meat slices into strips of thickness
2 mm (0.08 inches).
Lightly sauté the meat over a medium heat
so that some of the fat melts.
Cook the pasta al dente in boiling salted water.
Drain the pasta and add to the meat.
Sauté for a few moments, then turn off the heat.
Add the egg yolks and a ladleful of pasta water
and mix everything for about 30 seconds.
Add the remaining cheese, stir once again,
and serve immediately.
Garnish with freshly ground black pepper to taste.
This recipe can also be used with vermicelli pasta.

Preparation time: 10' + Cooking time: 8'
Difficulty: easy

VERMICELLI ALLA GRICIA

INGREDIENTS FOR 4 PEOPLE
300 g (0.66 lb) vermicelli pasta
150 g (0.33 lb) cured pork jowl or cured pork (bacon),
cut in small pieces
50 ml (3 1/2 tbsp) extra virgin olive oil
40 g (1.41 oz) pecorino romano cheese, grated
1 red chilli
salt and pepper

METHOD
Sauté the meat in the oil over a medium heat for 3 minutes
and add chilli to taste.
Meanwhile, cook the pasta al dente in boiling salted water.
Drain the pasta and add to the sauce.
Add the grated cheese and garnish with freshly ground
black pepper to taste.
This recipe can also be used with bucatini pasta.

Preparation time: 10' + Cooking time: 13'
Difficulty: easy

ZITI SPEZZATI
WITH 4 MEATS SAUCE

INGREDIENTS FOR 4 PEOPLE

300 g (0.66 lb) ziti pasta
150 g (0.33 lb) pork, cubed
100 g (0.22 lb) rabbit, cubed
100 g (0.22 lb) chicken breast, cubed
50 g (1.76 oz) turkey breast, cubed
50 ml (3 1/2 tbsp) white wine
50 g (1.76 oz) onion, cubed
50 g (1.76 oz) carrots, cubed
50 g (1.76 oz) celery, cubed
100 ml (1/3 cup + 1 1/2 tbsp) extra virgin olive oil
1 sprig rosemary
1 sprig sage
1 bay leaf
nutmeg
salt and pepper

METHOD

Sauté the vegetables over a medium heat in half the oil.
Add the meat to the vegetables and brown over a high heat,
until all the liquor has evaporated.
Add the wine and allow to evaporate.
Add the herbs and complete cooking, moistening
from time to time with a little water, if necessary.
Season with salt and pepper and flavour
with freshly ground nutmeg.
With a serrated knife, make two light incisions, crosswise, on
each of the pieces of pasta, so you can break them cleanly into
three parts. Cook the pasta al dente in boiling salted water.
Drain the pasta, add to the sauce and sauté with a little
of the pasta liquor. Stir in the remaining oil and serve.
This recipe can also be used with rigatoni pasta.

Preparation time: 1 h e 20' + Cooking time: 9'
Difficulty: easy

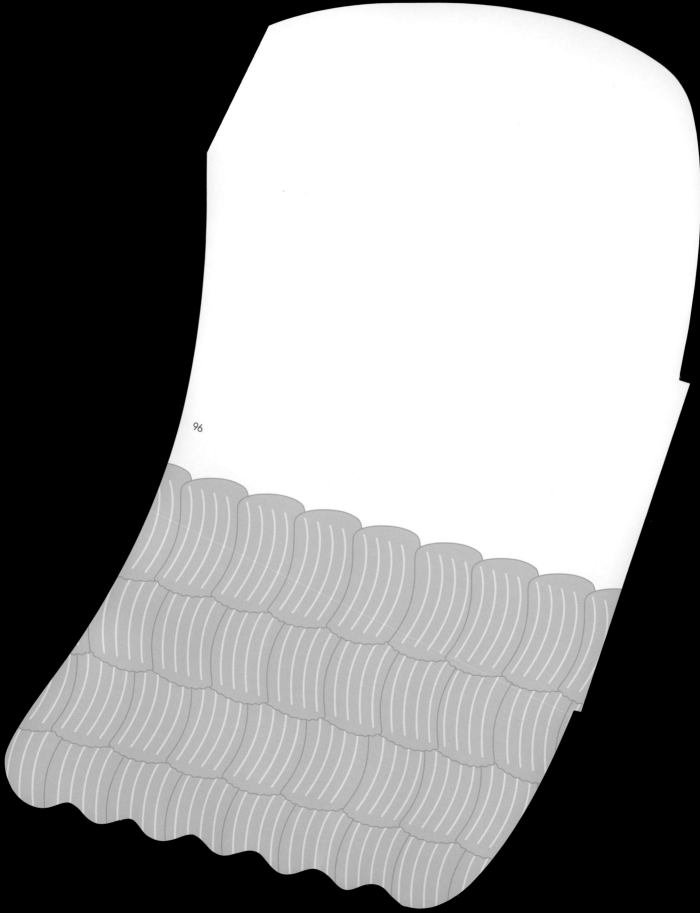

96

PASTA WITH CHEESE

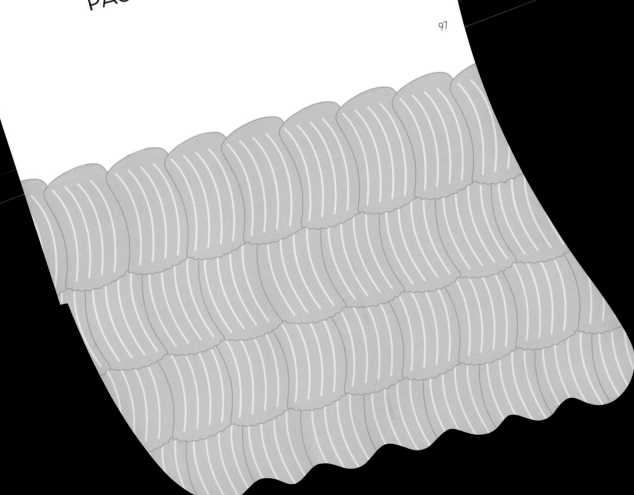

BUCATINI WITH CHEESE AND PEPPER

INGREDIENTS FOR **4** PEOPLE

300 g (0.66 lb) bucatini pasta
100 ml (1/3 cup + 1 1/2 tbsp) extra virgin olive oil
200 g (0.44 lb) pecorino romano cheese, grated
black, white and red pepper (coarsely ground)
salt

METHOD

Cook the pasta al dente in boiling salted water. Drain the pasta well. Off the heat, add the cheese, mixed with the oil and add 2 to 3 tablespoons of the pasta water. Lightly or generously dust coarsely ground black, white and red pepper to taste. For this recipe it is important that the pepper be coarsely ground. Serve immediately. This recipe can also be used with spaghetti.

Preparation time: 10' + Cooking time: 8'
Difficulty: easy

CASTELLANE WITH ARTICHOKES AND PECORINO

INGREDIENTS FOR **4** PEOPLE

300 g (0.66 lb) castellane pasta
4 artichokes, trimmed and not too thinly sliced
60 g (2.1 oz) shallots
60 g (2.1 oz) pecorino cheese, aged
50 ml (3 1/2 tbsp) dry white wine
50 ml (3 1/2 tbsp) vegetable stock
40 ml (3 tbsp) extra virgin olive oil
30 g (1 oz) parsley, chopped
1 garlic clove
1 red chilli
salt

METHOD

Gently sauté the artichoke slices in the oil, garlic, shallots, parsley, salt, chilli to taste and the wine.
Allow the liquor to completely evaporate and then add a little of the stock and complete the cooking (about 10 more minutes).
Cook the pasta al dente in boiling salted water.
Drain the pasta and add to the sauce.
Garnish with slices of the cheese.
This recipe can also be used with penne rigate pasta.

Preparation time: 45' + Cooking time: 9'
Difficulty: easy

CAVATELLI
ALLA CRUDAIOLA

INGREDIENTS FOR **4** PEOPLE
300 g (0.66 lb) cavatelli pasta
400 g (0.88 lb) tomatoes, seeded and cut in strips
120 g (0.26 lb) cacioricotta cheese, grated
80 ml (1/3 cup) extra virgin olive oil
8 basil leaves
1 garlic clove, minced
salt and pepper

METHOD
Marinate the tomatoes, in a refrigerator, with the olive oil,
basil, garlic and salt and pepper for 1 hour.
Cook the pasta al dente in boiling lightly salted water.
Drain the pasta and stir into the sauce.
Serve in pasta dishes and garnish with cheese.
This recipe can also be used with farfalle (bowtie) pasta.

102

Preparation time: 10' + Marinating time: 1 h + Cooking time: 9'
Difficulty: easy

SEMOLINA GNOCCHI WITH RICOTTA

INGREDIENTS FOR **4** PEOPLE
300 g (0.66 lb) semolina gnocchi
250 g (0.55 lb) very fresh ricotta cheese
100 g (3.5 oz) peas
60 g (2.1 oz) pecorino cheese, grated
salt and pepper

METHOD
Cook the peas for 1 minute in boiling salted water,
then drain and allow to cool in iced water.
Sieve the ricotta, allowing it to drop into a large mixing bowl,
then season with a pinch of salt and pepper.
Cook the pasta al dente in boiling salted water.
Drain the pasta, set aside a little of the liquor,
and add the pasta to the ricotta.
Stir in the grated cheese and the peas.
Mix all the ingredients together well.
If necessary, add a few tablespoons of the pasta water.
Serve the pasta quite hot.
This recipe can also be used with medium shells pasta.

Preparation time: 15' + Cooking time: 14'
Difficulty: easy

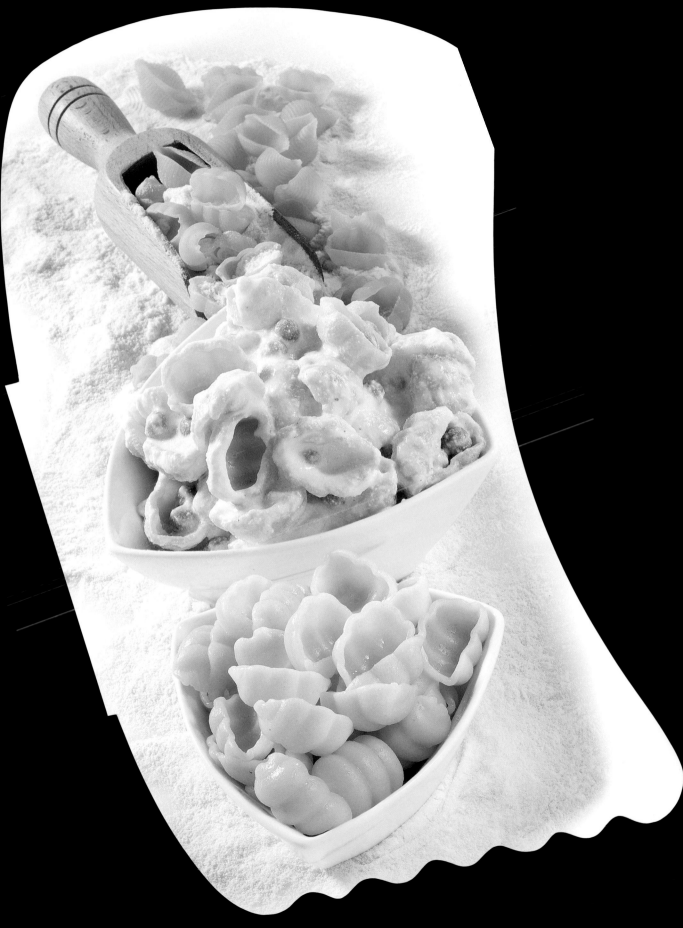

MARGHERITA-STYLE SALAD WITH CASTELLANE PASTA

INGREDIENTS FOR **4** PEOPLE
300 g (0.66 lb) castellane pasta
250 g (0.55 lb) cherry tomatoes
200 g (0.44 lb) mozzarella cheese
80 ml (1/3 cup) extra virgin olive oil
4 or 5 basil leaves, roughly torn
oregano (optional)
salt

METHOD
Cook the pasta al dente in boiling salted water. When still quite al dente, stop the cooking and cool the pasta quickly under cold running water, then drain thoroughly and pour into a large mixing bowl and drizzle with oil to prevent it sticking.
Cut the tomatoes into eight pieces and the mozzarella cheese into cubes of similar size.
Mix the tomatoes and mozzarella with the pasta.
Add a pinch of salt, the basil leaves and the oil. Serve.
If you like, you can garnish with a sprinkle of oregano.
This recipe can also be used with ruote pasta.

106

Preparation time: 15' + Cooking time: 12'
Difficulty: easy

MINI SHELLS SALAD WITH GORGONZOLA, PEAR AND WALNUT CREAM

INGREDIENTS FOR **4** PEOPLE

250 g (0.55 lb) mini shells pasta
250 g (0.55 lb) pears, cubed of side 1 cm (0.4 in)
150 g (0.33 lb) gorgonzola cheese, in small pieces
100 g (3 1/2 oz) full cream
10 ml (2 tsp) extra virgin olive oil
50 g (1.76 oz) walnut kernels
salt and pepper

METHOD

Cook the pasta al dente in boiling salted water. When cooked, stop the cooking and cool the pasta quickly under cold running water. Drain thoroughly and pour into a large mixing bowl. Add a drizzle of oil to prevent it sticking. Meanwhile, melt the cream and gorgonzola over a low heat. Add the pears (peeled if you wish) and the cream to the pasta. Break the walnuts into the mixture and season with salt and pepper.

This recipe can also be used with tortiglioni pasta.

Preparation time: 20' + Cooking time: 11'
Difficulty: easy

MEZZE PENNE ALLA NORMA

INGREDIENTS FOR **4 PEOPLE**

300 g (0.66 lb) mezze penne pasta
1 kg (2.2 lb) tomatoes, chopped
250 g (0.55 lb) eggplant, cubed or in batons
50 g (1.76 oz) onion, coarsely chopped
50 g (1.76 oz) salted ricotta, grated
30 ml (2 tbsp) extra virgin olive oil
6 basil leaves, roughly torn
1 garlic clove, peeled
flour
extra virgin olive oil for frying the eggplant
salt and pepper

METHOD

Arrange the eggplant in a colander and add salt so that the eggplant lets out its residual water.
After about 30 minutes, flour and fry the eggplant in oil.
Gently sauté the onion and garlic in the oil.
Add the tomatoes and season with salt and pepper.
Cook for about 10 minutes then pass the mixture through a vegetable mill. Add the eggplant to the sauce.
Meanwhile, cook the pasta al dente in boiling salted water.
Drain the pasta and add to the sauce with the basil.
Serve on pasta plates and garnish with ricotta.
This recipe can also be used with penne pasta.

Preparation time: 1 h + Cooking time: 11'
Difficulty: medium

PENNE RIGATE PICCOLE WITH CREAM OF ASPARAGUS AND PARMIGIANO-REGGIANO

INGREDIENTS FOR **4 PEOPLE**

300 g (0.66 lb) penne rigate piccole pasta
450 g (1 lb) asparagus, trimmed
100 ml (1/3 cup + 1 1/2 tbsp) full cream
100 g (3.5 oz) parmigiano-reggiano cheese, grated
30 g (1 oz) shallots, sliced
20 ml (1 tbsp + 1 tsp) extra virgin olive oil

METHOD

Gently sauté the shallots in the oil until brown. Set aside the asparagus tips and slice the rest then add the slices to the shallots and sauté for 2 minutes. Cover with 0.5 litres of water and cook for about 15 minutes.

Salt lightly and blend to a cream.

Blanch the asparagus tips for 3 to 4 minutes then cool immediately in iced water.

Cook the pasta al dente in boiling salted water as per the packet instructions. Drain the pasta and add to the cream.

Add the asparagus tips, the full cream and the cheese.

Mix everything together over a low heat for 1 minute before serving.

This recipe can also be used with mezze penne pasta.

Preparation time: 30' + Cooking time: 9'
Difficulty: easy

PIPETTE RIGATE WITH CAULIFLOWER

INGREDIENTS FOR 4 PEOPLE

300 g (0.66 lb) pipette rigate pasta
650 g (1.43 lb) cauliflower florets
100 g (3.5 oz) ricotta cheese, aged and flaked
30 ml (2 tbsp) extra virgin olive oil
20 g (0.7 oz) parsley, chopped
3 anchovy fillets, in oil
1 garlic clove, peeled
1 red chilli
salt

METHOD

Cook the cauliflower in boiling salted water for about 10 minutes. Meanwhile, gently sauté the garlic and chilli over a low heat. Add the anchovy fillets, taking care they do not burn. Drain the cauliflower and add to the anchovy. Cook for 5 minutes over a medium heat, adding a few spoons of water from the cauliflower liquor if it becomes too dry. Mash the cauliflower with a fork (or blend it for a creamier consistency). Cook the pasta al dente in boiling salted water. Drain the pasta and add to the cream. Mix everything well over heat for 1 and then add the parsley. Garnish with ricotta. This recipe can also be used with tortiglioni pasta.

Preparation time: 15' + Cooking time: 8'
Difficulty: easy

TORTIGLIONI WITH 4 CHEESES

INGREDIENTS FOR 4 PEOPLE

300 g (0.66 lb) tortiglioni pasta
100 g (3.5 oz) gorgonzola cheese, cubed
100 g (3.5 oz) provolone cheese, cubed
100 g (3.5 oz) parmigiano-reggiano cheese, grated
100 g (3.5 oz) fontina cheese, cubed
150 ml (2/3 cup) milk
50 ml (3 1/2 tbsp) full cream
salt and pepper

METHOD

Gently heat all the cheeses, except the parmigiano-reggiano, with the milk over a low heat, allowing them to melt and stir until creamy. Meanwhile, cook the pasta al dente in boiling salted water. Drain the pasta and add to the cheese along with the cream. Season to taste with salt and freshly ground pepper. Stir over heat for 2 minutes so that the cheese sauce mixes with the pasta. Add a little of the pasta water if the sauce becomes too thick.
This recipe can also be used with semolina gnocchi.

116

Preparation time: 15' + Cooking time: 12'
Difficulty: easy

WHOLE-GRAIN TORTIGLIONI WITH CAPRINO AND DRIED TOMATOES

INGREDIENTS FOR **4** PEOPLE

300 g (0.66 lb) whole-grain tortiglioni pasta
200 g (0.44 lb) fresh caprino cheese
60 g (2.1 oz) dried tomatoes, cut in thin strips
20 g (0.7 oz) green olives, pitted and chopped
10 g (0.3 oz) salted capers
20 ml (1 tbsp + 1 tsp) extra virgin olive oil
2 or 3 basil leaves, roughly torn
dried oregano
salt

METHOD

Cook the pasta al dente in boiling salted water as per the packet instructions. Meanwhile, rinse the capers under running water, drain and chop coarsely. Add the cheese to a large bowl and dilute with a ladleful of the pasta liquor then mix to a cream. Add the capers, olives and tomato. Season with salt and flavour with a pinch of oregano.
When the pasta is cooked, drain it and add to the cream. Mix everything well then add the oil and basil.
This recipe can also be used with penne rigate pasta.

Preparation time: 10' + Cooking time: 11'
Difficulty: easy

TROFIE LIGURI WITH PESTO

INGREDIENTS FOR 4 PEOPLE

300 g (0.66 lb) trofie liguri pasta
30 g (1 oz) basil leaves
60 g (2.1 oz) parmigiano-reggiano cheese, grated
40 g (1.41 oz) pecorino cheese, aged and grated
10 g (0.3 oz) pine nuts
1 garlic clove
200 ml (3/4 cup + 1 1/2 tbsp) extra virgin olive oil
(preferably Ligurian)
salt

METHOD

Blend the basil, 150 ml (2/3 cup) of oil, a pinch of salt,
garlic and pine nuts.
Add the cheeses to get a pesto. Cover the pesto
with the remaining oil and set aside.
Cook the pasta al dente in boiling salted water.
Drain the pasta and add to the pesto.
Mix well, adding a little of the pasta liquor
and a drizzle of oil.
This recipe can also be used with farfalle (bowtie) pasta.

Preparation time: 15' + Cooking time: 10'
Difficulty: easy

ALPHABETICAL
INDEX OF RECIPES

ALPHABETICAL
INDEX OF INGREDIENTS

ACADEMIA BARILLA
AMBASSADOR OF ITALIAN
GASTRONOMY THROUGHOUT THE WORLD

In the heart of Parma, one of the most distinguished capitals of Italian cuisine, is the Barilla Center. Set in the grounds of the former Barilla pasta factory, this modern architectural complex is the home of Academia Barilla. This was founded in 2004 to promote the art of Italian cuisine, protecting the regional gastronomic heritage and safeguarding it from imitations and counterfeits, while encouraging the great traditions of the Italian restaurant industry. Academia Barilla is also a center of great professionalism and talent that is exceptional in the world of cooking. It organizes cooking classes for culinary enthusiasts, it provides services for those involved in the restaurant industry, and it offers products of the highest quality. In 2007, Academia Barilla was awarded the "Premio Impresa-Cultura" for its campaigns promoting the culture and creativity of Italian gastronomy throughout the world. The center was designed to meet the training requirements of the world of food and it is equipped with all the multimedia facilities necessary for organizing major events. The remarkable gastronomic auditorium is surrounded by a restaurant, a laboratory for sensory analysis, and various teaching rooms equipped with the most modern technology. The Gastronomic Library contains over 10,000 books and a remarkable collection of historic menus as well as prints related to culinary subjects. The vast cultural heritage of the library can be consulted on the internet which provides access to hundreds of digitized historic texts. This avant-garde approach and the presence of a team of internationally famous experts enables Academia Barilla to offer a wide range of courses, meeting the needs of both restaurant chefs and amateur food lovers. In addition, Academia Barilla arranges cultural events and activities aiming to develop the art of cooking, supervised by experts, chefs, and food critics, that are open to the public. It also organizes the "Academia Barilla Film Award", for short films devoted to Italy's culinary traditions.

www.academiabarilla.com

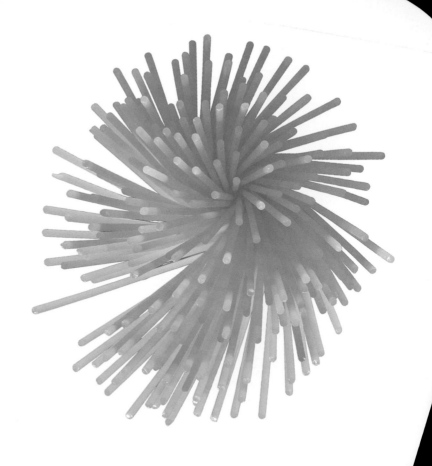

WHITE STAR PUBLISHERS

WS White Star Publishers® is a registered trademark
property of De Agostini Libri S.p.A.

© 2013 De Agostini Libri S.p.A.
Via G. da Verrazano, 15
28100 Novara, Italy
www.whitestar.it - www.deagostini.it

Translation: John Venerella

ISBN 978-88-544-0726-8
2 3 4 5 6   17 16 15 14 13

Printed in China

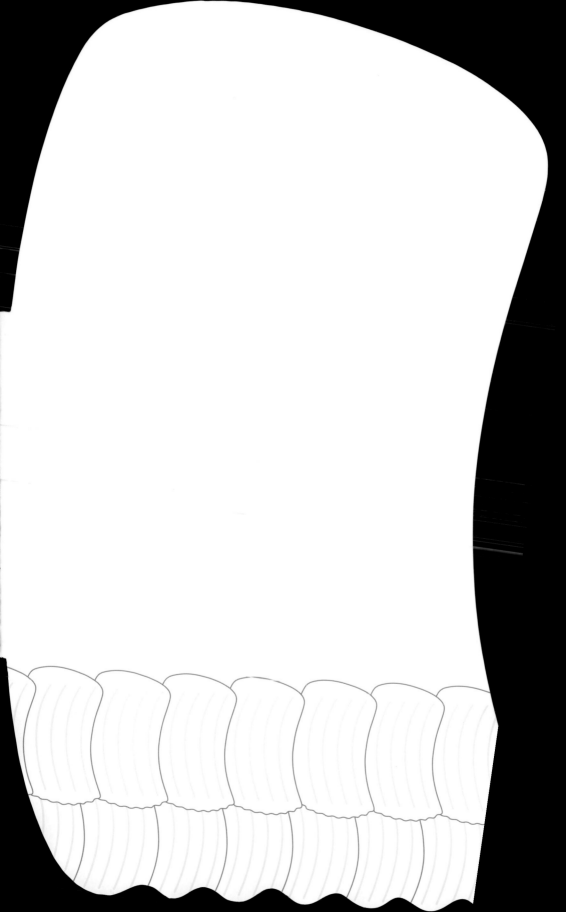

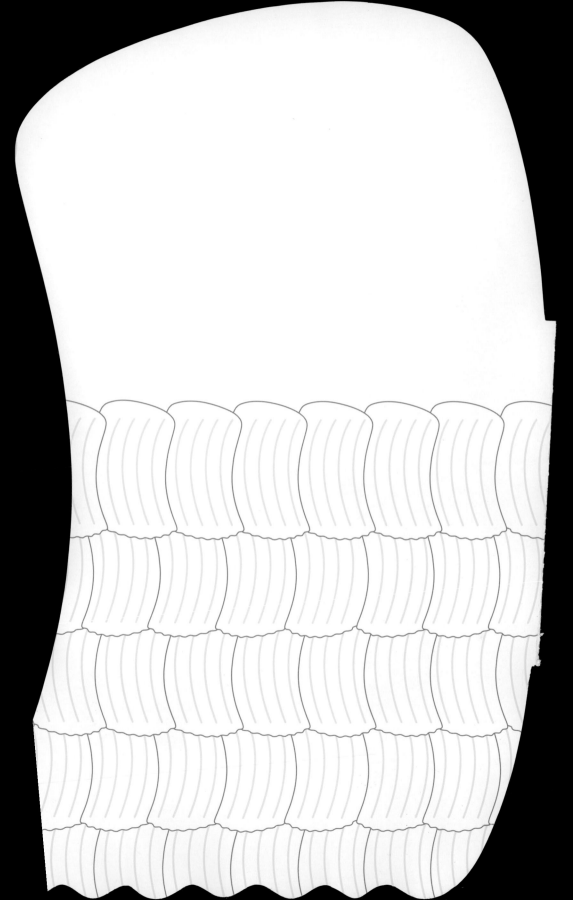